The Tailor and the Crow:

An Old Rhyme
with
New Drawings

by
L. Leslie Brooke

[ZHINGOORA BOOKS]

THE TAILOR AND THE CROW

A carrion crow sat on an oak,
Fol de riddle, lol de riddle, hi ding do,

Watching a tailor shape his cloak;

Sing heigh ho,

the carrion crow,

Fol de riddle,

lol de riddle,

hi ding do.

Wife,

bring me my old bent bow,

Fol de riddle,

lol de riddle,

hi

ding do.

That I may shoot yon carrion crow;

Sing heigh ho, the carrion crow,

Fol de riddle, lol de riddle, hi ding do.

The tailor he shot

and missed his mark,

Fol de riddle,

lol de riddle,

hi ding

do.

And shot his own sow quite through the heart;

Sing heigh ho, the carrion crow,
Fol de riddle, lol de riddle, hi ding do.

Wife, bring brandy in a spoon,

Fol de riddle,

lol de riddle,

hi-ding do.

For our old sow

is in a swoon;

Sing

HEIGH

HO,

the carrion crow,

Fol de riddle, lol de riddle, hi ding

do.

The End

www.ingramcontent.com/pod-product-compliance
Lightning Source LLC
Chambersburg PA
CBHW060014300526
45794CB00003B/1190